INSTANT VORTEX AIR FRYER OVEN FOR VEGETARIAN

With Love By
Catherine B. Roberts

Disclaimer Notice:

Please note the information contained within this document is for educational and entertainment purposes only. All effort has been executed to present accurate, up to date, and reliable, complete information. No warranties of any kind are declared or implied. Readers acknowledge that the author is not engaging in the rendering of legal, financial, medical or professional advice. The content within this book has been derived from various sources. Please consult a licensed professional before attempting any techniques outlined in this book.

By reading this document, the reader agrees that under no circumstances is the author responsible for any losses, direct or indirect, which are incurred as a result of the use of information contained within this document, including, but not limited to, — errors, omissions, or inaccuracies.

Table Of Contents

INTRODUCTION

As a mom and a food lover, I have used many different kinds of appliances for cooking. But my favorite appliance is the Instant Vortex Air Fryer Oven. You can cook different foods in it and it is very easy to use.

I don't have to spend a lot of time cooking and cleaning. I just turn on the oven and it does all the work for me.

Many people find cooking to be hard and time-consuming. They make the same recipes over and over again.

Do you find it hard to decide what to cook? You can buy a kit with all the ingredients you need, or order meat and vegetables from a restaurant. Both are easy and quick.

Restaurant food is bad for your health and it is expensive. And with meal kits, there are no opportunities to be creative.

Cooking your own food at home is a good idea because you can make the food and control what ingredients go into it.

The time you spend cooking will not be long. You can use easy recipes and the Instant Vortex so that you don't need to spend much time on it.

Breakfasts, lunch, appetizers and desserts. You can make them if you are a meat eater or vegetarian. There is something for everyone here.

The best part of these recipes is that you can make them as healthy or unhealthy as you want. You might be very hungry when reading the recipe, but don't worry.

This book is not for people who are very careful with their food. These recipes make it okay to eat some of the food you like, but if you are on a diet, there may be tips you can learn from this book.

If the diet says you can, then you can have a cheat day. You can enjoy food that is not healthy. Let's move on to see what this air fryer oven tastes like.

I enjoy cooking and creating recipes so much that I do it for a hobby.

I was thin when I was a child. Some foods I could eat without thinking of the calories. For example, onion rings, french fries, donuts and chicken fingers are fried foods.

I like these foods the most. I usually eat them when we go out to a restaurant. But now that I am getting older, I know that this is not good for me anymore.

I got fat. It was hard to lose weight. I know that you need to give up the things you love to eat. So, I ate less often at restaurants and gave away my deep-fryer in order to get more control over what I ate.

I did not enjoy my food because I could not eat what I wanted.

One day, I tried to fry things with air. I saw commercials for these machines. People always ask me if they work.

I was a little confused about the air fryer. It can cook food without all the mess. I wanted to try it anyway, but I was not sure if it would work.

I was scared to try it, but I tried it anyway. First, I tried chicken strips that were my favorite. When I tasted them they were good.

Air frying food is good because it tastes as good as food cooked with oil. It is less bad for me, and the food tastes better to me too. I like this way of cooking, so now I cook with air fryer.

After I used the Instant Vortex for a little while, I realized that it was a good way to make food. It is easy and quick. You can make small quantities of any kind of food with it.

Now that my kids are grown, they don't eat with me. I used to cook for them when they were little. Now I only cook for myself and my husband sometimes. Cooking for one or two people is really easy with the help of my Instant Vortex!

I love my air fryer. It is perfect for when I want to make a meal for myself and my husband or when friends are over.

The Instant Vortex is a machine we can use when we are camping. It helps us make food that tastes like at home even when we are camping. I love the Instant Vortex because it is easy to use and makes my favorite foods too!

All of the recipes in this book are easy to make. If you make them, they will taste good and if you have Instant Vortex, it will be even easier for you. Let's see more about it!

6 Reasons Why I Love Instant Vortex

Whether you are new to air fryers or not, this book is for you. It has recipes and tips for cooking and creativity.

If you are new to cooking, this book has many good recipes to make. More experienced cooks might find some new take on the classics that they have been making for years.

I hope you will use these recipes and love them. They can help you get a lot of good food fast.

1.Instant Vortex is good for healthy and cheap food. I can make a nutritious meal because it's fast. I don't eat out as much because Instant Vortex is healthy and cheap.

2. Instant Vortex is better for you than regular frying.

Deep fried foods have a lot of calories. There are 9 calories in each gram of fat from deep fried foods. This can make it hard to keep your calories low, but you can still eat deep fried food if you want to and make smarter choices in the rest of what you eat.

The instant vortex is magical because it makes you lose weight by reducing the number of calories you eat.

3. Instant Vortex is the best way to keep your kitchen clean. You will not need many dishes. You can put it in the air fryer and then cook it with a few bowls, so you do not need any big pots or pans.

4. The Vortex has no limits. You can make anything that you would usually cook in an oven, like appetizers like fried mozzarella sticks, to main dishes like honey baked ham, to desserts like chocolate cakes. Instant Vortex helps you make easy, healthy recipes. It is a new way to think about food that is quick and good for your body.

5. When you have All in One Appliance, you can cook with Air Fry, Broil, Bake and Reheat. There are also Rotate buttons that help for rotisserie-style cooking.

GET CREATIVE

Small kitchen appliances are helpful for us. I created every recipe in this book to save you time and money. I want your meals to be enjoyable, too.

The ingredients list is short and there are not a lot of steps to prepare the food. This book is also a source of inspiration for cooking what you like.

Instant Vortex makes cooking easy. You can change the recipes to make less food or more food, it is so versatile.

This bundle of recipes will show you how easy it is to make breakfast, side dishes, main dishes, and desserts. I am sure you will like the recipes I have made for Instant Vortex.

Panko Beans

Servings: 4   Prep Time: 7 Min   Cooking Time: 15 Minutes

Ingredients:

½ cup flour

2 eggs

1 cup panko bread crumbs

½ cup grated Parmesan cheese

1 teaspoon cayenne pepper

Salt and black pepper, to taste

1½ pounds (680 g) green beans

Directions:

In a bowl, put the flour. In another bowl, beat the eggs. In another shallow bowl, mix the bread crumbs with cheese, cayenne pepper, salt and pepper. Dip the green beans in flour then in beaten eggs then in bread crumbs.

Put the green beans into the basket. Put the air fryer basket on a pan. Set it on Rack Position 2, and set the temperature to 400 F for 15 minutes. Stir halfway through cooking time. When done, put them in a bowl and serve.

Nutrition: Calories: 690   Protein: 7.3g   Carbs: 6.4g Fat: 17.5g

Mushroom Club Sandwich

Servings: 4   Prep Time: 12 Min   Cooking Time: 25 Minutes

Ingredients:

¼ tbsp. red chili sauce

½ cup water

2 slices of white bread 1 tbsp. softened butter

¼ tbsp. Worcestershire sauce

½ tsp. olive oil

½ flake garlic crushed

¼ cup chopped onion

1 cup minced mushroom

1 small capsicum

Directions:

Take the bread and cut it. Then put the ingredients for the sauce on top of it and wait for it to thicken. Add mushrooms to the sauce. When they cook, stir them so they get all of the flavor from everything else in there. Put some capsicum on a cookie sheet and let it cook until roasted, then take the skin off.

Cut the peppers into slices. Put sauce on the pepper. Turn up the oven to 300 degrees Fahrenheit for 5 minutes and put a basket of bread in it. Put two pieces of bread in one spot so they don't touch each other.

Please keep the fryer on for 15 minutes around 250 degrees. Turn the Classic Sandwiches after 3 minutes and then again at 15 minutes. Serve with a sauce, such as tomato ketchup or mint sauce.

Nutrition: Calories 287 Fat 7.8 g Carbs 48 g Protein 17.9 g

Meatloaf For You

Servings: 8   Prep Time: 7 Min   Cooking Time: 65 Minutes

Ingredients:

Nonstick cooking spray

3 1/3 cups chickpeas, cooked

1 onion, chopped fine

2 stalks celery, chopped

2 carrots, chopped fine

2 cloves garlic diced fine

2 cups panko bread crumbs

½ cup almond milk, unsweetened

3 tbsp. vegan Worcestershire sauce

3 tbsp. soy sauce, divided

2 tbsp. olive oil

2 tbsp. flax seeds, ground

¼ cup + 2 tbsp. tomato paste

1 tsp liquid smoke

¼ tsp pepper

2 tbsp. maple syrup

2 tbsp. apple cider vinegar

1 tsp paprika

Directions:

Place the rack in position. Lightly spray a 9-inch loaf pan with cooking spray. Put chickpeas, onion, celery, carrots, cloves, bread crumbs, milk and soy sauce into a food processor. You may need to do this in batches.

Mix the ingredients but don't over blend. Put the mix in a bowl and mix. Then put into a pan and then bake it. Set your oven to 375°F for 35 minutes, add the pan to the oven, and then bake for 30 minutes or until done.

In a small bowl, mix the tomato paste, soy sauce, syrup, vinegar and paprika together. When the timer goes off in 20-25 minutes, take out the loaf and put glaze on it. Let it cool 10 minutes before cutting and serving.

Nutrition: Calories 625, Fat 11g Carbs 82g Protein 23g

Roasted Vegetables Salad

Servings: 5   Prep Time: 5 Min   Cooking Time: 1 hr 30 Minutes

Ingredients:

3 eggplants

1 tbsp of olive oil

3 medium zucchini

1 tbsp of olive oil

4 large tomatoes, cut them in eighths

4 cups of one shaped pasta

2 peppers of any color

1 cup of sliced tomatoes cut into small cubes

2 teaspoon of salt substitute

8 tbsp of grated parmesan cheese

½ cup of Italian dressing Leaves of fresh basil

Directions:

To Prepare: Wash your eggplant and slice it. Do not peel the eggplant. Slice into 1/2 inch thick rounds. Toss with olive oil in the air fryer oven for about 8 minutes or until browned and crisp.

Cook the eggplants in a pot for 40 minutes. Place the pot on a stove and set it to 360 degrees Fahrenheit. While that cooks, wash your zucchini and cut it into thick slices with the green end off but do not peel it first. Cut your zucchini into rounds of ½ inch each thickness.

Add 1 tbsp of olive oil to your ingredients. Cook the zucchini for 25 minutes on a 360° F heat. Wash and cut the tomatoes. Put them in a basket and put them in an air fryer oven for 30 minutes.

When the timer is off, set it at 350 degrees Fahrenheit. Cook pasta according to instructions. Use cold water to wash the pasta and drain it.

Meanwhile, wash the peppers. Chop them and put them in a bowl. Wash the cherry tomatoes and cut them into thin slices and put them in the bowl with the peppers. Add your roasted veggies to the bowl. Add pasta, salt to taste, and dressing on top of it all. Then add basil on top before tossing everything together.

Mix with your hands, set the ingredients together in the refrigerator, and let it chill Serve your salad and enjoy it!

Nutrition: Calories: 160 Protein: 4.1g Carbs: 18.4g Fat: 8.3g

Cauliflower Bites

Servings: 4   Prep Time: 10 Min   Cooking Time: 18 Minutes

Ingredients:

1 Head Cauliflower, cut into small florets Tsps Garlic Powder Pinch of Salt and Pepper

1 Tbsp Butter, melted 1/2 Cup Chili Sauce Olive Oil

Directions:

Put the cauliflower in a bowl and pour some oil over. Season it with salt, pepper, and garlic powder. Then mix it up really well with your hands. Put the florets in an air fryer oven at 350 degrees for 14 minutes.

Remove the cauliflower from the oven. Pour melted butter with chili sauce over the cauliflower, so it is well coated. Put in the oven for 3-4 minutes. Serve as a side or with ranch or cheese dip as a snack!

Nutrition: Calories 402 Fat 14.5 g Carbs 25.2 g Protein 45.9 g

Veggie & Garlic Bake

Servings: 4   Prep Time: 5 Min   Cooking Time: 20 Minutes

Ingredients:

1 lb turnips, sliced

1 large red onion, cut into rings

1 large zucchini, sliced

Salt and black pepper to taste

2 cloves garlic, crushed

1 bay leaf, cut in 6 pieces

1 tbsp olive oil

Directions:

Place the turnips, onion, and zucchini in a bowl. Put some oil on them and add salt and pepper. Turn up the Instant Vortex to 330 degrees Fahrenheit. Put them all in a pan with cooking spray.

Put the bay leaves in different parts of the slices. Put garlic cloves in between them. Then press Start and cook for 15 minutes. Serve with a meat dish or a salad.

Nutrition: Calories 247 Fat 2.4 g Carbs 12.3 g Protein 44.3 g

Roasted Bell Peppers With Garlic

Servings: 4   Prep Time: 10 Min   Cooking Time: 22 Minutes

Ingredients:

1 green bell pepper, sliced into 1-inch strips

1 red bell pepper, sliced into 1-inch strips

1 orange bell pepper, sliced into 1-inch strips

1 yellow bell pepper, sliced into 1-inch strips

2 tablespoons olive oil, divided

½ teaspoon dried marjoram

Pinch salt

Freshly ground black pepper, to taste

1 teaspoon garlic minced

Directions:

Put some olive oil in a large bowl. Put the bell peppers inside and mix them up with the olive oil. Add some marjoram, salt, and pepper to taste. Mix again and put them aside. Cut off the top of the head of garlic, place it on a piece of aluminum foil, then wrap it.

Drizzle the top with the remaining 1 tablespoon of olive oil and wrap the garlic cloves in foil. Transfer the garlic to the air fryer basket. Put the air fryer basket on the baking pan and slide into Rack Position 2, select Roast, set temperature to 330°F and set time to 15 minutes.

After 15 minutes, take the peppers out of the oven and add them. Cook for 7 more minutes and then they will be cooked and finished.

Remove the garlic and unwrap the foil. Let it rest for awhile. Take out of the skin once cooled and put on a plate with bell peppers. Stir together, then eat!

Nutrition: Calories 252 Fat 2.4 g Carbs 12.2 g Protein 44.3 g

Okra Flat Cakes

Servings: 2   Prep Time: 10 Min   Cooking Time: 20 Minutes

Ingredients:

2 or 3 green chilies finely chopped

1 ½ tbsp. lemon juice

Salt and pepper to taste

2 tbsp. garam masala

2 cups sliced okra

3 tsp. ginger finely chopped

1-2 tbsp. fresh coriander leaves

Directions:

Mix the ingredients in a bowl. Add water to make it less hard. Heat up your oven at 160 degrees for 5 minutes and put the okra in.

1. You can cook the French Cuisine Galettes in the fry basket. Cook them for another 25 minutes at the same temperature, rolling them over to get a uniform cook.

2. Then you can serve it with either mint sauce or ketchup.

Nutrition: Calories 458 Carbs 40.7g Fat 22.7g Protein 43.5g

Vegan Beetroot Chips

Servings: 2   Prep Time: 6 Min   Cooking Time: 9 Minutes

Ingredients:

4 cups golden beetroot slices

2 tbsp olive oil

1 tbsp yeast flakes

1 tsp vegan seasoning Salt to taste

Directions:

Put oil, beetroot, vegan seasoning, and yeast in a bowl. Mix well. Put chips in basket. Set the oven to 370 degrees F and press Start. Cook for 14-16 minutes on AirFry function shaking once halfway through cooking time. Serve

Nutrition: Calories 445 Fat 32.5 g Carbs 0.7 g Protein 35.4 g

Cayenne Tahini Kale

Servings: 3 or 4   Prep Time: 10 Min   Cooking Time: 15 Minutes

Ingredients:

¼ cup tahini

¼ cup fresh lemon juice

2 tablespoons olive oil

1 teaspoon sesame seeds

½ teaspoon garlic powder

¼ teaspoon cayenne pepper

4 cups packed torn kale leaves (stems and ribs removed and leaves torn into palm-size pieces)

Kosher salt and freshly ground black pepper, to taste

Directions:

Make the dressing. Put tahini, lemon juice, olive oil, sesame seeds, garlic powder and cayenne pepper in a bowl. Mix it until it is mixed well. Add the kale and mix it with the dressing. Sprinkle salt and pepper to season.

Put the kale leaves on the air fryer basket. Put it in a baking pan. Set the heat to 350°F (180°C). Cook for 15 minutes. When it is done, the leaves will be slightly wilted and crispy.

Remove from the oven and serve on a plate.

Nutrition: Calories: 321 Protein: 3g   Carbs: 12.7g   Fat: 31.3g

Cheesy Cabbage Wedges

Servings: 4   Prep Time: 5 Min   Cooking Time: 25 Minutes

Ingredients:

½ head cabbage, cut into wedges

2 cups Parmesan cheese, chopped

4 tbsp melted butter

Salt and black pepper to taste

½ cup blue cheese sauce

Directions:

You can coat the cabbage wedges with butter and mozzarella cheese. Put them in a greased basket and put it in a baking sheet. Cook for 20 minutes at 380 F degrees on an air fry setting. Serve with blue cheese sauce.

Nutrition: Calories: 388 Fat: 16.2 g Carbs: 42.0 g Protein: 23.0 g.

Black Gram French Cuisine Galette

Servings: 6   Prep Time: 20 Min   Cooking Time: 30 Minutes

Ingredients:

2 or 3 green chilies finely chopped

1 ½ tbsp. lemon juice

Salt and pepper to taste

2 cup black gram

2 medium potatoes boiled and mashed

1 ½ cup coarsely crushed peanuts

3 tsp. ginger finely chopped

1-2 tbsp. fresh coriander leaves

Directions:

Mix the ingredients in a clean bowl. Then, make the mixture into round and flat French Cuisine Galettes. Wet them slightly with water. Turn on the Instant Vortex oven at 160 degrees Fahrenheit for 5 minutes.

First, put the French Cuisine Galettes on a fry basket and let them cook for 25 more minutes. They will be done when they are brown and crispy. Turn them over to make sure they cook evenly. Serve with either mint sauce or ketchup.

Nutrition: Calories 174 Fat 8g Carbs 14g Protein 16g

Cabbage Flat Cakes

Servings: 6   Prep Time: 22 Min   Cooking Time: 30 Minutes

Ingredients:

2 or 3 green chilies finely chopped

1 ½ tbsp. lemon juice

Salt and pepper to taste

2 tbsp. garam masala

2 cups halved cabbage leaves

3 tsp. ginger finely chopped

1-2 tbsp. fresh coriander leaves

Directions:

Mix the ingredients in a bowl. Add water to it. Make sure that you use enough to cover the cabbage. Turn on the oven at 160 degrees Fahrenheit for five minutes before you put the paste on.

To make the French Cuisine Galettes, put them in a fry basket and cook for 25 minutes at the same temperature. Keep rolling them over to make sure they are cooked evenly. Serve with either mint sauce or ketchup.

Nutrition: Calories: 324 Protein: 3g   Carbs: 12.7g   Fat: 31.3g

Cayenne Spicy Green Beans

Servings: 4   Prep Time: 5 Min   Cooking Time: 20 Minutes

Ingredients:

1 cup panko breadcrumbs

2 whole eggs, beaten

½ cup Parmesan cheese, grated

½ cup flour

1 tsp cayenne pepper

1 ½ pounds green beans

Salt to taste

Directions:

In a bowl, mix panko breadcrumbs with Parmesan cheese. Add salt, pepper, and cayenne pepper. Roll the green beans in flour and dip them in eggs. Dredge them in the parmesan-panko mix.

Put the beans in a cooking basket that is greased. Put it in a baking tray and cook for 15 minutes at 350 degrees Fahrenheit. Shake the beans once while they are cooking. Serve them and enjoy!

Nutrition: Calories 176 Fat 8.1g Carbs 0.3g Protein 23.8g

Asian-Inspired Broccoli

Servings: 2   Prep Time: 10 Min   Cooking Time: 10 Minutes

Ingredients:

12 ounces (340 g) broccoli florets

2 tablespoons Asian hot chili oil

1 teaspoon ground Sichuan peppercorns (or black pepper)

2 garlic cloves, finely chopped

1 (2-inch) piece fresh ginger, peeled and finely chopped

Kosher salt and freshly ground black pepper

Directions:

Toss the broccoli with a little chili oil, some Sichuan peppercorns, garlic and ginger. Season it with salt and pepper. Put the broccoli in an air fryer basket and cook for 10 minutes at 390 degrees Fahrenheit.

Put the air fryer basket on a baking pan. Slide it into Rack Position 2. Select Air Fry and set the temperature to 375 degree F. Set the cooking time to 10 minutes and stir halfway through cooking time.

When the broccoli is done, it should be lightly brown. It should also be tender. Then you can take it out and put it on a plate to serve.

Nutrition: Calories: 255 Protein: 13.1g Carbs: 10.4g Fat: 7.5g

Gherkins Flat Cakes

Servings: 4   Prep Time: 10 Min   Cooking Time: 12 Minutes

Ingredients:

2 or 3 green chilies finely chopped

1 ½ tbsp. lemon juice

Salt and pepper to taste

2 tbsp. garam masala

2 cups sliced gherkins

3 tsp. ginger finely chopped

1-2 tbsp. fresh coriander leaves

Directions:

Put the ingredients in a bowl. Mix it with water. The dough should not be too thick or too thin and should be able to spread easily on the gherkin. Heat up the Instant Vortex oven at 160 degrees Fahrenheit for 5 minutes before you put anything in there.

Place the Galettes in the fry basket. Cook them for 25 minutes at 325 degrees. Keep turning them over to get an even cook and make sure they are cooked all the way through. Serve with ketchup or mint sauce!

Nutrition: Calories: 248 Protein: 37.2g Carbs: 9.4g   Fat: 7.1g

Mint French Cuisine Galette

Servings: 6   Prep Time: 17 Min   Cooking Time: 20 Minutes

Ingredients:

1-2 tbsp. fresh coriander leaves

2 or 3 green chilies finely chopped

1 ½ tbsp. lemon juice

Salt and pepper to taste

2 cups mint leaves (Sliced fine)

2 medium potatoes boiled and mashed

1 ½ cup coarsely crushed peanuts

3 tsp. ginger finely chopped

Directions:

Mix the sliced mint leaves with the other ingredients in a bowl. Make round and flat food like French Cuisine Galettes. Wet them with water (put some water on your hands and then rub it onto the food). Then, put crushed peanuts on each one.

Put the French Cuisine Galettes in the Instant Vortex oven for 5 minutes at 160 degrees Fahrenheit. Turn them over every 25 minutes and cook for another 25 minutes. Serve with mint sauce or ketchup.

Nutrition : Calories 232 Fat 20.1 g Carbs 30.1 g Protein 14.6 g

Cottage Cheese French Cuisine Galette

Servings: 6   Prep Time: 15 Min   Cooking Time: 20 Minutes

Ingredients:

1-2 tbsp. fresh coriander leaves

2 or 3 green chilies finely chopped

1 ½ tbsp. lemon juice

Salt and pepper to taste

2 tbsp. garam masala

2 cups grated cottage cheese

1 ½ cup coarsely crushed peanuts

3 tsp. ginger finely chopped

Directions:

In a clean bowl, mix the ingredients. Make them into round and flat shapes. Wet the French Cuisine Galettes slightly with water. Coat each French Cuisine Galette with crushed peanuts. Turn on your oven to 160 degrees Fahrenheit for 5 minutes

Place the French Cuisine Galettes in the fry basket. Cook them for another 25 minutes at the same temperature, rolling them over. Serve with mint sauce or ketchup.

Nutrition: Calories: 334 Carbs: 39.6g Protein: 3.8g Fat: 17.9g

Stuffed Portobello Mushrooms With Vegetables

Servings: 4   Prep Time: 10   Cooking Time: 8 Minutes

Ingredients:

4 portobello mushrooms, stem removed

1 tablespoon olive oil

1 tomato, diced

½ green bell pepper, diced

½ small red onion, diced

½ teaspoon garlic powder

Salt and black pepper, to taste

½ cup grated Mozzarella cheese

Directions:

Using a spoon to scoop out the gills of the mushrooms and discard them. Brush the mushrooms with olive oil. In a bowl, mix together all of the other ingredients except for Mozzarella cheese.

Stuffing each mushroom with the filling and putting cheese on it. Put the mushrooms in a basket, put them on a pan, set the temperature to 330°F and time to 8 minutes. When cooking is done, the cheese will be melted. Serve warm.

Nutrition: Calories 401 Fat 8 g Carbs 10 g Protein 23 g

Radish Flat Cakes

Serves 2   Prep time: 15 minutes   Cook time: 37 minutes

Ingredients:

1-2 tbsp. fresh coriander leaves

2 or 3 green chilies finely chopped

1 ½ tbsp. lemon juice

Salt and pepper to taste

2 tbsp. garam masala

2 cups sliced radish

3 tsp. ginger finely chopped

Directions:

Mix the ingredients in a clean bowl. Add water to it so that the paste is not too watery. Heat up your Instant Vortex oven at 160 degrees Fahrenheit for 5 minutes.

Place the French Cuisine Galettes in a fry basket and cook for 25 more minutes. Keep rolling them over to get an even cook. Serve with either mint sauce or ketchup.

Nutrition: Calories 247 Fat 15.7 g Carbs 0.4 g Protein 24.8 g

Cottage Cheese Gnocchi's

Serves 6   Prep time: 5 minutes   Cook time: 10 minutes

Ingredients:

2 tsp. ginger-garlic paste

2 tsp. soya sauce

2 tsp. vinegar

1 ½ cup all-purpose flour

½ tsp. salt

5 tbsp. water

2 cups grated cottage cheese

2 tbsp. oil

Directions:

First, wrap the dough and put it in the fridge. Then cook the filling for your pizza. Make sure you cover the cottage cheese with sauce. After that, roll out your dough and put it on a pizza dish with the filling in the middle.

Now, wrap the dough around the filling and pinch the edges together. Heat up your oven to 200° F for 5 minutes. Place the gnocchi's in a fry basket and close it. Let them cook at this temperature for another 20 minutes.

Recommended sides are chili sauce or ketchup.

Nutrition: Calories 212 Fat 6.6 g Carbs 7.2 g Protein 31.7 g

Stuffed Mushrooms

Servings: 12   Prep Time: 5 Min   Cooking Time: 8 Minutes

Ingredients:

2 Rashers Bacon, Diced

½ Onion, Diced

½ Bell Pepper, Diced

1 Small Carrot, Diced

24 Medium Size Mushrooms (Separate the caps & stalks)

1 cup Shredded Cheddar Plus Extra for the Top

½ cup Sour Cream

Directions:

Chop the mushrooms finely and fry them up with bacon, onion, pepper and carrot. Fry for 8 minutes at 350 ° F. When the vegetables are fairly tender, stir in sour cream and cheese.

Heat the cheese until it melts. Put some filling on the mushroom caps. Then put them in the fryer basket and top with some more cheese.

Nutrition: Calories 292 Fat 8g Protein 17g Carbs 36g

Cottage Cheese Fingers

Serves 6   Prep time: 15 minutes   Cook time: 1 hour

Ingredients:

2 tsp. salt

1 tsp. pepper powder

1 tsp. red chili powder

6 tbsp. corn flour

4 eggs

2 cups cottage cheese

Oregano fingers

2 cup dry breadcrumbs

2 tsp. oregano

1 ½ tbsp. ginger-garlic paste

4 tbsp. lemon juice

Directions:

Mix all the ingredients for the marinade. Put the chicken in a dish and let it rest overnight. Mix breadcrumbs, oregano and red chili flakes together and place the chicken on top of this mixture. Cover it with plastic wrap until you are ready to cook it.

Pre heat your oven to 160 degrees Fahrenheit for 5 minutes. Put the Oregano Fingers in the fry basket and close it. Let them cook at this temperature for 15 more minutes or so. Shake up the Oregano Fingers so that they are cooked evenly on all sides.

Nutrition: 299 Calories 16g Fat 4g Carbs 16g Protein

Cheesy Frittata With Vegetables

Servings: 2   Prep Time: 10 min   Cooking Time: 25 Minutes

Ingredients:

1 cup baby spinach

½ cup sliced mushrooms

1 zucchini, sliced with a 1-inch thickness

1 small red onion, sliced

¼ cup chopped chives

¼ lb asparagus, trimmed and sliced thinly

2 tsp olive oil

4 eggs, cracked into a bowl

½ cup milk

Salt and black pepper to taste

½ cup grated Cheddar cheese

½ cup crumbled Feta cheese

Directions:

Preheat the oven to 320 F. Put parchment paper in a baking dish. Mix the eggs, milk, salt and pepper together. Heat some oil on a stove over medium heat and add vegetables like asparagus, zucchini, onion, mushrooms and baby spinach for 5 minutes.

Pour the veggies into the baking dish. Cover with egg mixture. Add feta and cheddar cheese on top. Cook for 15 minutes or until done. Garnish with chives.

Nutrition: Calories: 387 Fat: 8g Carbs: 4g Protein: 18g

Lemony Brussels Sprouts And Tomatoes

Servings: 4   Prep Time: 5 Min   Cooking Time: 20 Minutes

Ingredients:

1 pound (454 g) Brussels sprouts, trimmed halved

1 tablespoon extra-virgin olive oil

Salt

black pepper, to taste

½ cup sun-dried tomatoes, chopped

2 tablespoons freshly squeezed lemon juice

1 teaspoon lemon zest

Directions:

Line the air fryer basket with aluminum foil. Toss Brussels sprouts with olive oil in a large bowl. Sprinkle with salt and black pepper. Put the Brussels sprouts in a single layer in the basket and put it on the baking pan. Set temperature to 400°F (205°C) and set time to 20 minutes

When you are done, the Brussels sprouts should be caramelized. Remove them from the oven to a serving bowl along with the tomatoes. Add lemon juice and lemon zest. Toss with those ingredients. Serve immediately.

Nutrition: Calories 412 Fat 11.1 g Carbs 38.8 g Protein 38.9 g

Cheese-Walnut Stuffed Mushrooms

Servings: 4   Prep Time: 10 Cooking Time: 10 Minutes

Ingredients:

4 large portobello mushrooms 1 tablespoon canola oil

½ cup shredded Mozzarella cheese ⅓ cup minced walnuts

2 tablespoons chopped fresh parsley

Cooking spray

Directions:

Wipe the cooking spray on the basket. Remove the mushroom stems and spoon out the gills that are inside with a spoon. Coat each mushroom with canola oil and then top them with shredded Mozzarella cheese, followed by walnuts.

Put the air fryer basket on a baking pan and slide it into rack position 2. Put the temperature to 350 F and set time to 10 minutes. When cooking is finished, the mushrooms should be golden brown. Then take them out of the oven and put them on a plate with parsley for garnish before serving.

Nutrition: Calories: 696   Protein: 17.5g Carbs: 6.4g   Fat: 17.5g

Cilantro Roasted Carrots With Cumin Seeds

Servings: 4   Prep Time: 5 Min   Cooking Time: 15 Minutes

Ingredients:

1 lb carrots, julienned

1 tbsp olive oil

1 tsp cumin seeds

2 tbsp fresh cilantro, chopped

Directions:

Preheat the Instant Vortex on AirFry function to 350 F. Add oil and cumin seeds to a bowl and mix them together with the carrots. Make sure that all of the carrots are coated in oil. Place them on a baking tray with star markings, and cook for 10 minutes. Scatter fresh coriander over the carrots

Nutrition: Calories 642 Fat 56.5g Carbs: 5.7g Protein 28.5g

Spinach Enchiladas With Mozzarella

Servings: 4   Prep Time: 10 Min   Cooking Time: 20 Minutes

Ingredients:

8 corn tortillas, warm

2 cups mozzarella cheese, shredded

1 cup ricotta cheese, crumbled

1 package frozen spinach

1 garlic clove, minced

½ cup sliced onions

½ cup sour cream

1 tbsp butter

1 can enchilada sauce

Directions:

In a pan, add oil and cook the garlic and onion for 3 minutes. Add the spinach and cook for 5 more minutes. Remove from pan and mix in some ricotta cheese, sour cream, and mozzarella. Spoon ¼ cup of the mixture onto a tortilla.

Put the tortilla in the basket. Repeat with all of the rest of the tortillas. Pour the sauce on, and add cheese to taste before cooking it for 15 minutes at 380 degrees Fahrenheit.

Nutrition: Calories 301 Fat 15.3g Carbs 10.9g Protein 17.1g

Cottage Cheese Spicy Lemon Kebab

Servings: 4   Prep Time: 10 Min   Cooking Time: 10 Minutes

Ingredients:

3 tsp. lemon juice

2 tbsp. coriander powder

3 tbsp. chopped capsicum

2 tbsp. peanut flour

2 cups cubed cottage cheese

3 onions chopped

5 green chilies-roughly chopped

1 ½ tbsp. ginger paste

1 ½ tsp. garlic paste

1 ½ tsp. salt

3 eggs

Directions:

Put corn flour on the cottage cheese cubes. Mix the other ingredients together in a bowl and make it into a smooth paste. Coat the cheese cubes with that mixture and put them in the refrigerator for an hour. Beat eggs and add salt to them, then dip the cornmeal-covered cheese cubes in this mix for ten seconds each time and put in the refrigerator for 1 hour.

Preheat the oven to 290 Fahrenheit for around 5 minutes. Place the kebabs in a basket and cook them for 25 more minutes at this temperature. Turn the kebabs over halfway through cooking, so they will be cooked evenly on both sides. Serve with mint sauce.

Nutrition: Calories: 471 Protein: 13.8g Carbs: 19.9g Fat: 11.1g

White Lentil French Cuisine Galette

Serves 6   Prep time: 15 minutes   Cook time: 15 minutes

Ingredients:

1 ½ tbsp. lemon juice

Salt and pepper to taste

2 cup white lentil soaked

3 tsp. ginger finely chopped

1-2 tbsp. fresh coriander leaves

2 or 3 green chilies finely chopped

Directions:

Wash the soaked lentils and mix it with the rest of the ingredients in a clean bowl. Mold this mixture into round and flat French Cuisine Galettes. Wet the French Cuisine Galettes slightly with water. Pre heat the Instant Vortex oven at 160 degrees Fahrenheit for 5 minutes.

Place the French Cuisine Galettes in the fry basket and let them cook for another 25 minutes at the same temperature. Keep rolling them over to get a uniform cook. Serve either with mint sauce or ketchup.

Nutrition: Calories 160 Fat 8.1 g Carbs 1.2 g Protein 21.7 g

Air Fried Winter Vegetables

Servings: 2   Prep Time: 5Min   Cooking Time: 16 Minutes

Ingredients:

1 parsnip, sliced

1 cup sliced butternut squash

1 small red onion, cut into wedges

½ chopped celery stalk

1 tablespoon chopped fresh thyme

2 teaspoons olive oil

Salt and black pepper, to taste

Directions:

Put all the ingredients in a large bowl. Stir well. Put the vegetables on the air fryer basket. Slide it onto a baking pan and put it into Rack Position 2 of the air fryer. Set temperature to 380°F (193°C) and set time to 16 minutes.

Stir the vegetables halfway through the cooking time. When the vegetables are done, they should be golden brown and tender. Then you can eat them!

Nutrition: Calories 168 Fat 4.3 g Carbs 10.5 g Protein 20.6 g

Tortellini With Veggies And Parmesan

Servings: 4   Prep Time: 5 Min   Cooking Time: 16 Minutes

Ingredients:

8 ounces (227 g) sugar snap peas, trimmed

½ pound (227 g) asparagus, trimmed and cut into 1-inch pieces

salt

1 tablespoon extra-virgin olive oil

1½ cups water

1 (20-ounce / 340-g) package frozen cheese tortellini

2 garlic cloves, minced

1 cup heavy (whipping) cream

1 cup cherry tomatoes, halved

½ cup grated Parmesan cheese

¼ cup chopped fresh parsley or basil

Put the peas and the asparagus in a bowl. Add salt and olive oil. Mix it up until everything is well coated. Put them in a baking pan.

Directions:

Slide your pan into the oven. Set the temperature to 450°F and set the timer for 4 minutes. Mix 1 teaspoon of salt with water. Take out your food when it is cooked, then put it in the pan with tortellini.

Pour the water over the tortellini. Put the pan back to the oven. Slide it in Rack Position 1, select Convection Bake, set temperature to 450 degrees Fahrenheit and set time for 7 minutes.

While cooking, mix together the garlic, cream, and salt. Take the pan out when it is done. Wipe off any remaining oil on the outside of the pan with a towel.

Stir the ingredients in the pan. Pour the cream over and put tomatoes on top. Put it in Rack Position 2, select Roast, set the temperature to 375 F, and set the timer for 5 minutes.

After four minutes, take the casserole out of the oven. Add Parmesan cheese and stir until it melts. Top with parsley.

Nutrition: Calories 451 Fat 20 g Carbs 20.9 g Protein 44.9 g

Chili Cottage Cheese

Servings: 4   Prep Time: 5 Min   Cooking Time: 16 Minutes

Ingredients:

2 tbsp. olive oil

1 capsicum. Cut into thin and long pieces (lengthwise).

2 small onions. Cut them into halves.

1 ½ tsp. ginger garlic paste.

½ tbsp. red chili sauce.

2 tbsp. tomato ketchup.

1 ½ tbsp. sweet chili sauce.

2 tsp. vinegar.

2 tsp. soya sauce.

A few drops of edible red food coloring.

1-2 tbsp. honey.

2 cups cubed cottage cheese

2 ½ tsp. ginger-garlic paste

1 tsp. red chili sauce

¼ tsp. salt

¼ tsp. red chili powder/black pepper

A few drops of edible orange food coloring

¼ tsp. Ajinomoto. A pinch of black pepper powder.

1-2 tsp. red chili flakes.

For the garnish, use the greens of spring onions and sesame seeds.

Directions:

To make the cubes of cottage cheese, mix them with something. Coat the chicken well. Preheat the oven at 250 Fahrenheit for 5 minutes or more. Put some Oregano Fingers in the fryer and then heat it up too.

Now let the fryer stay at 290 Fahrenheit for 20 minutes more. Toss the Oregano Fingers periodically through the cook to get a uniform cook.

Add the ingredients to the sauce. Cook them with the vegetables until it thickens. Add the Oregano Fingers (herbs) and cook it longer.

Nutrition: Calories 168 Fat 4.2 g Carbs 10.5 g Protein 20.6 g

Vegetable Spicy Lemon Kebab

Servings: 2   Prep Time: 7 Min   Cooking Time: 20 Minutes

Ingredients:

1 ½ tsp. salt

3 tsp. lemon juice

2 tsp. garam masala

4 tbsp. chopped coriander

3 tbsp. cream

3 tbsp. chopped capsicum

2 cups mixed vegetables

3 onions chopped

5 green chilies-roughly chopped

1 ½ tbsp. ginger paste

1 ½ tsp. garlic paste

3 eggs

2 ½ tbsp. white sesame seeds

Directions:

Mix the ingredients except for the egg and make a paste. Coat the vegetables with that. Now, stir eggs with salt in it and dip the coated vegetables in it. Then transfer to the sesame seeds and coat the vegetables well.

Put the vegetables on a stick to bake them in an oven that is 160 degrees Fahrenheit for 25 minutes.

Turn the sticks over in between the cooking process to get a uniform cook.

Nutrition: Calories 162 Fat 8.1 g Carbs 1.2 g Protein 21.7 g

Mushroom Marinade Cutlet

Serves 6   Prep time: 10 minutes Cook time: 15 minutes

Ingredients:

2 cup fresh green coriander

½ cup mint leaves

4 tsp. fennel

2 tbsp. ginger-garlic paste

1 small onion

6-7 flakes garlic (optional)

Salt to taste

2 cups sliced mushrooms

1 big capsicum (Cut this capsicum into big cubes)

1 onion (Cut it into quarters. Now separate the layers carefully.)

5 tbsp. gram flour

A pinch of salt to taste

3 tbsp. lemon juice

Directions:

Put the coriander, mint, fennel, and ginger into a clean container. Add the onion/garlic and salt. Squeeze some lemon juice in. Stir them together until they are mixed well. Put this mixture into a grinder and grind them until they are a thick paste. Slit the mushrooms nearly to the end and leave them apart.

Take the mushroom and put the paste inside. Put some sauce on top of it. Put some flour and salt in the sauce. Mix it together well. Then rub this mixture all over the mushroom so that it is completely covered with a brown color.

Now, to the leftover sauce, add the capsicum and onions.

Put the sauce on each piece of capsicum and onion. Now take satay sticks and put pieces of cottage cheese and vegetables on them. Preheat the Instant Vortex oven at 290 Fahrenheit for around 5 minutes.

Open the basket. Arrange the satay sticks properly.

Put the mushrooms on the stick and make sure that they will cook at 180 degrees for 30 minutes. Leave the veggies on a different stick, but make sure they are cooking at 180 degrees for 7 minutes.

Turn the sticks in between so that one side does not get burnt and also to provide a uniform cook.

Nutrition: Calories: 251 Protein: 13.2g Carbs: 10.4g Fat: 7.5g

Winter Vegetarian Frittata

Servings: 4   Prep Time: 10 Min   Cooking Time: 30 Minutes

Ingredients:

1 leek, peeled and thinly sliced into rings

2 cloves garlic, finely minced

3 medium-sized carrots, finely chopped

2 tablespoons olive oil

6 large-sized eggs

Sea salt and ground black pepper, to taste

1/2 teaspoon dried marjoram, finely minced

1/2 cup yellow cheese of choice

Directions:

First, cook the leek, garlic and carrot in hot olive oil. When they are cooked, put them to the side. Next you will use your Instant Vortex air fryer oven to heat it up to 330 degrees F.

In a bowl, mix eggs with salt, pepper and marjoram. Grease the inside of your baking dish with a nonstick cooking spray. Pour the mixed eggs into the baking dish.

Stir in the carrots and cheese. Put them into the oven. Cook for about 30 minutes, then serve.

Nutrition: 297 Calories 16g Fat 4g Carbs 16g Protein

Asian Tofu "meatballs"

Servings: 4   Prep Time: 10 Min   Cooking Time: 10 Minutes

Ingredients:

3 dried shitake mushrooms

Nonstick cooking spray

14 oz. firm tofu, drained & pressed

¼ cup carrots, cooked

¼ cup bamboo shoots, sliced thin

½ cup Panko bread crumbs

2 tbsp. corn starch

3 ½ tablespoon soy sauce, divided

1 tsp garlic powder

¼ tsp salt

1/8 tsp pepper

1 tbsp. olive oil

2 tbsp. garlic, diced fine

2 tbsp. ketchup

2 tsp sugar

Directions:

Place the shitake mushrooms in a bowl and add just enough water to cover. Let soak 20 minutes until soft. Drain well and chop. Place the baking pan in position Lightly spray the fryer basket with cooking spray.

Put the tofu, carrots, bamboo shoots, bread crumbs, corn starch and soy sauce in a food processor. Mix until combined. Then take some of the mixture and shape it into 1-inch balls.

Put balls in the fryer basket. You might need to cook them in batches. Put them in the oven on 380°F for 10 minutes, and turn them halfway through cooking. Cook garlic on medium heat for 1 minute, then pour it over the balls.

Add soy sauce, ketchup and sugar to the sauce. Let the meatballs cook in the sauce for 3-5 minutes. Put them on top of rice or noodles if you want.

Nutrition: Calories 309 Fat 12g Carbs 28g Protein 20g

Cottage Cheese And Mushroom Mexican Burritos

Serves 8   Prep time: 2 hours 15 minutes   Cook time: 30 minutes

Ingredients:

½ cup mushrooms thinly sliced

1 cup cottage cheese cut in too long and slightly thick Oregano Fingers A pinch of salt to taste

½ tsp. red chili flakes

1 tsp. freshly ground peppercorns

½ cup pickled jalapenos

1-2 lettuce leaves shredded

½ cup red kidney beans (soaked overnight)

½ small onion chopped 1 tbsp. olive oil

2 tbsp. tomato puree

¼ tsp. red chili powder

1 tsp. of salt to taste

4-5 flour tortillas

1 or 2 spring onions chopped finely.

Also cut the greens.

Take one tomato. Remove the seeds and chop it into small pieces. 1 green chili chopped.

1 cup of cheddar cheese grated

1 cup boiled rice (not necessary)

A few flour tortillas to put the filing in

Directions:

Put onion and garlic in a pan to cook. Do the same with beans. Mash them together. Add sauce to taste before putting it in the burrito.

To make the filling, cook it in a pan. That way the vegetables taste good. To make the salad, put all of the ingredients together in a bowl and mix them up.

Put the tortilla on a plate. Put sauce, beans, and filling in the middle. Then put salad on top of all that. Turn your oven on for 5 minutes at 200 Fahrenheit before you roll it up.

Open the fry basket and keep the burritos inside. Close the basket properly. Let the Air Fryer remain at 200 Fahrenheit for 15 more minutes. Halfway through, take out the basket and turn all of the burritos over to get a uniform cook.

Nutrition: 246 Calories 22g Fat 5g Carbs 8g Protein

Maple And Pecan Granola

Servings: 4   Prep Time: 12 Min   Cooking Time: 20 Minutes

Ingredients:

1½ cups rolled oats

¼ cup maple syrup

¼ cup pecan pieces

1 teaspoon vanilla extract

½ teaspoon ground cinnamon

Directions:

Line a baking sheet with parchment paper. Mix together oats, maple syrup, pecan pieces, vanilla and cinnamon in a bowl until the oats and pecan pieces are completely covered.

Make the mixture. Put it in a pan. Put the pan on the first rack, set the oven to 300 degrees, and set it for 20 minutes. Check on it halfway through and stir it then.

When you are finished cooking, cool for 30 minutes. The granola might still be a little soft, but as it cooks more it will become firm.

Nutrition: Calories 248 Fat 11.9 g Carbs 1.8 g Protein 35 g

Mushroom Pops

Servings: 4   Prep Time: 5 Min   Cooking Time: 35 Minutes

Ingredients:

1 tsp. dry basil

1 tsp. lemon juice

1 tsp. red chili flakes

1 cup whole mushrooms

1 ½ tsp. garlic paste

Salt

pepper to taste

1 tsp. dry oregano

Directions:

Add the ingredients to a bowl and mix them together. Now, dip the mushrooms into this mixture and wait some time. Put your oven on when it is 180°C for 5 minutes.

Place the cheese in the fryer basket. Cook for 20 more minutes with the same temperature. Keep turning them over so they are cooked evenly. Serve with tomato ketchup on top.

Nutrition: Calories: 351   Protein: 25g   Carbs: 5.8g   Fat: 14g

Vegetable Au Gratin

Servings: 3   Prep Time: 5 Min   Cooking Time: 30 Minutes

Ingredients:

1 cup cubed eggplant

¼ cup chopped red pepper

¼ cup chopped green pepper

¼ cup chopped onion

½ cup chopped tomatoes

1 clove garlic, minced

1 tbsp sliced pimiento-stuffed olives

1 tsp capers

¼ tsp dried basil

¼ tsp dried marjoram

Salt

black pepper

¼ cup grated mozzarella cheese

1 tbsp breadcrumbs

Directions:

In a bowl, put eggplant, peppers, onion, tomatoes, olives, garlic, basil and marjoram. Add salt and black pepper. Grease a baking tray with cooking spray. Add the vegetables to the tray and spread them evenly.

Put cheese on top of the dish. Put bread crumbs over that. Cook it in your Instant Vortex for 20 minutes on the Bake function at 360 degrees Fahrenheit. Serve it!

Nutrition: Calories 247 Fat 2.6 g Carbs 12.2 g Protein 44.3 g

Tasty Polenta Crisps

Servings: 4   Prep Time: 15 Min   Cooking Time: 25 Minutes + Chilling Time

Ingredients:

2 cups milk

1 cup instant polenta

Salt and black pepper to taste fresh thyme, chopped

Directions:

Put water and milk in a pan. Put the pan on low heat. Stir it with a whisk. Pour in the polenta, and keep stirring until it thickens and bubbles. Add salt to taste.

Add polenta to a baking tray. Put it in the fridge for 45 minutes or until you can slice it. Cut the polenta into small lengths, and then bake them in an oven at 350 degrees Fahrenheit for 25 minutes; cook for 16 minutes at 380 F on Air Fry function, turning once halfway through. Make sure the fries are golden and crispy. Serve.

Nutrition: Calories 729 Carbs 5.4 g Protein 73.1g Fat 45.9g

Cauliflower Spicy Lemon Kebab

Serves 4   Prep time: 1 hr 10 minutes Cook time: 14 minutes

Ingredients:

3 tsp. lemon juice

2 tsp. garam masala

3 eggs

2 ½ tbsp. white sesame seeds

2 cups cauliflower florets

3 onions chopped

5 green chilies-roughly chopped

1 ½ tbsp. ginger paste

1 ½ tsp. garlic paste

1 ½ tsp. salt

Directions:

Put the ingredients in a bowl, but do not put the egg. Then mix it all together and make it into a paste. Dip the florets in the paste and then dip them in beaten eggs and salt, too. Put sesame seeds on them so they are covered with it well.

Put the vegetables on a stick. Put the sticks in the basket and let them cook for 25 minutes at 160 degrees Fahrenheit.Turn the sticks over in between the cooking process to get a uniform cook.

Nutrition: Calories: 284Protein: 26g   Carbs: 35g   Fat: 25g

Cottage Cheese Best Homemade Croquette

Servings: 4   Prep Time: 8 Min   Cooking Time: 30 Minutes

Ingredients:

1 big capsicum (Cut this capsicum into big cubes)

1 onion (Cut it into quarters. Now separate the layers carefully.)

5 tbsp. gram flour

A pinch of salt to taste

2 cup fresh green coriander

½ cup mint leaves

4 tsp. fennel

1 small onion

2 tbsp. ginger-garlic paste

6-7 garlic flakes (optional)

3 tbsp. lemon juice

2 cups cottage cheese cut into slightly thick and long pieces (similar to French fries)

Salt

Directions:

Put coriander, mint, fennel, and ginger into a container. Put salt and lemon juice on them. Mix them up. Pour this into a grinder and blend until you get a thick paste. Put the cottage cheese pieces in too.

Cut these pieces in half and leave them in the middle. Now stuff all of the pieces with the paste that you made. Leave it alone so it can dry out.

Take the sauce and mix in some flour and salt. Rub this mixture all over the stuffed cottage cheese pieces. Leave the cottage cheese aside now.Now, to the leftover sauce, add the capsicum and onions.

Put sauce on the vegetable and the onion. Now put sticks of cottage cheese and vegetables on separate sticks.

Pre heat the Instant Vortex oven at 290 Fahrenheit for around 5 minutes. Open the basket.

Put the sticks with cheese at 180 degrees for about half an hour. Put the other ones at 180 degrees for 7 minutes.

Turn the sticks in between so that one side does not get burnt and also to provide a uniform cook.

Nutrition: Calories 726 Carbs 5.3 g Protein 73.1g Fat 45.9g

Feta & Scallion Triangles

Servings: 4   Prep Time: 5 Min   Cooking Time: 20 Minutes

Ingredients:

4 oz feta cheese, crumbled

2 sheets filo pastry

1 egg yolk, beaten

2 tbsp fresh parsley, finely chopped

1 scallion, finely chopped

2 tbsp olive oil

Salt

black pepper

Directions:

In a bowl, mix the yolk with cheese, parsley, and scallion. Season with salt and black pepper. Cut each filo sheet in 3 strips. Put a teaspoon of the feta mixture on the bottoms of all three pieces of filo dough and then stack them together to make a triangle shape.

Put the dough on a rolling pin. Roll it into a circle. Put the filling in the center of that circle. Now, roll it up until you get to the top and seal it off with your fingers. Turn on Instant Vortex at 350 degrees Fahrenheit, then put in for about 10 minutes or until done.

Brush the surface of filo with oil. Put up to 5 pieces in the oven and press start. Cook for 5 minutes at 330 F, then lower the temperature to 300 F and cook for 3 more minutes until it is golden brown.

Nutrition: Calories: 287 Protein: 25g   Carbs: 35g   Fat: 25g

Traditional Jacket Potatoes

Servings: 4   Prep Time: 5 Min   Cooking Time: 30 Minutes

Ingredients:

4 potatoes, well washed

2 garlic cloves, minced

Salt and black pepper to taste

1 tsp rosemary

1 tsp butter

Directions:

First you need to preheat the oven at 360 degrees. Poke the potatoes with a fork. Put them in your basket and put it inside of the thing that also has a baking tray. Cook for 25 minutes.

Cut the potatoes in half. Put butter and some rosemary on them. Season with salt and pepper. Serve it right away!

Nutrition: Calories 475 Fat 16.4 Carbs 1.9 g Protein 59.6 g

Veggie Mix Fried Chips

Servings: 4   Prep Time: 5 Min   Cooking Time: 45 Minutes

Ingredients:

1 large eggplant, cut into strips

5 potatoes, peeled and cut into strips

3 zucchinis, cut into strips

½ cup cornstarch

½ cup olive oil

Salt to taste

Directions:

Preheat the Instant Vortex on the AirFry function to 390 F. In a bowl, stir together cornstarch, ½ cup of water, salt, pepper, olive oil and eggs. Put in this mixture vegetables like eggplants and zucchini. Put vegetables in the basket and press Start. Cook for 12 minutes. Serve

Nutrition : Calories 234 Fat 21.1 g Carbs 30.1 g Protein 14.6 g

Ratatouille

Servings: 6   Prep Time: 20 Min   Cooking Time: 12 Minutes

Ingredients:

1 medium zucchini, sliced ½-inch thick

1 small eggplant, peeled and sliced ½-inch thick

2 teaspoons kosher salt, divided

4 tablespoons extra-virgin olive oil, divided

3 garlic cloves, minced

1 small onion, chopped

1 small red bell pepper, cut into ½-inch chunks

1 small green bell pepper, cut into ½-inch chunks

½ teaspoon dried oregano

¼ teaspoon freshly ground black pepper

1 pint cherry tomatoes

2 tablespoons minced fresh basil

1 cup panko bread crumbs

½ cup grated Parmesan cheese (optional)

Directions:

Season the zucchini and eggplant with salt. Put them on a rack, salted side down, on a baking sheet. Sprinkle the other sides with salt too.

Let the zucchini and eggplant slices sit for 10 minutes. When they have water coming out, rinse them and then cut them into quarters or eighths.

Pour the zucchini and eggplant, 2 tablespoons of olive oil, garlic, onion, bell peppers, oregano, and black pepper into a bowl. Toss to coat them well. Put the vegetable mixture in the air fryer basket.

Put the air fryer basket onto a baking pan. Slide it into Rack Position 2. Select Roast and set the temperature to 375°F. Set your time to 12 minutes. Then add the tomatoes and basil to the large bowl.Sprinkle with the remaining ½ teaspoon of salt and 1 tablespoon of olive oil.

Toss the pasta with olive oil, Parmesan cheese, and panko. Put it in the oven for 6 minutes. Take it out and put some tomato sauce on top. Stir them together so they are mixed well.

Put the panko on top. Put in the oven for 6 minutes. It is done when it is brown. Cool for 5 minutes before you serve it.

Nutrition: Calories: 387 Fat: 8g Carbs: 4g Protein: 18g

Roasted Vegetables With Rice

Servings: 4   Prep Time: 10 Min   Cooking Time: 12 Minutes

Ingredients:

2 teaspoons melted butter

1 cup chopped mushrooms

1 cup cooked rice

1 cup peas

1 carrot, chopped

1 red onion, chopped

1 garlic clove, minced

Salt and black pepper, to taste

2 hard-boiled eggs, grated

1 tablespoon soy sauce

Directions:

Butter the baking pan with butter. Mix together the mushrooms, rice, peas, carrots, onion, garlic and salt and pepper in a bowl. Put this mixture into the pan.

Turn the rack to position two and set the oven to 380 degrees, or as hot as it goes. Cook for 12 minutes. When the cooking is done, take the pan out. Put some of the mixture on each plate and have dinner!

Serve warm with a sprinkle of grated eggs and a drizzle of soy sauce.

Nutrition: Calories 380 Cal Fat 125.11 g Carbs 10 g Protein 87.9 g

Butter Burgers

Servings: 4   Prep Time: 10 Min   Cooking Time: 30 Minutes

Ingredients:

Nonstick cooking spray

½ cup black beans, rinsed & drained

12 oz. mushrooms, sliced

1 ½ cup brown rice, cooked

½ cup oats 1 tsp salt

½ tsp pepper

1 tsp garlic powder

1 tsp onion powder

¼ tsp red pepper flakes

¼ cup Vegan butter

2 cups onions, sliced

Directions:

Place the baking pan in the oven. Lightly spray the fryer basket with cooking spray. Pat dry beans with paper towel to remove all of the water from them. Heat a medium skillet over medium-high heat and add oil to it.

Add mushrooms and cook, stirring frequently, until almost no moisture remains.

Nutrition: Calories: 255 Protein: 13.1g Carbs: 10.4g Fat: 7.5g

Functions of Vortex Air Fryer Oven

The Vortex Air Fryer Oven comes with a touch screen LED display and various functions that are used during the

The vortex air fryer has a touch panel that is digital. You can use it to cook your food automatically or manually.

7 Different Smart Programs/Function Modes

The smart programs are automated. They are programmed to do things like set the time or temperature. When you use these functions you never need to set them yourself. When the oven goes into standby mode, it will display "OFF". These smart programs are:

1. Air Fry

2. Broil

3. Roast

4. Bake

5. Dehydrate

6. Reheat

Start

The Start button is used to start the cooking process.

Cancel

As the name suggests, when you press cancel, it will stop your cooking. When you press cancel, it will stop your cooking and then go on standby mode.

Light

The Light button is used to turn ON and OFF the oven light. After 5 minutes of time oven light turn OFF automatically.

(+ / -) Temperature Controls (Temp)

The (+) button is used to make the temperature higher and the (-) button is used to make the temperature lower.

(+ / -) Time

You can use the (+ / -) time button to change the cooking time on your stove. To increase cooking time, touch and hold "+". To decrease cooking time, touch and hold "-".

Rotate

When you start the cooking process, the Rotate button will turn on. You just need to touch it once more to stop the rotisserie. This button is only available when you choose Air Fry or Roast in the cooking process. When the key turns blue, then it means that you can use it.

CPSIA information can be obtained
at www.ICGtesting.com
Printed in the USA
BVHW050608260122
627123BV00005B/429